A Photographic Guide to the History of the Shadow Puppet Theatre in the West

by

Max von Boehn

Copyright © 2011 Read Books Ltd.
This book is copyright and may not be
reproduced or copied in any way without
the express permission of the publisher in writing

British Library Cataloguing-in-Publication Data
A catalogue record for this book is available from
the British Library

OCCIDENTAL SHADOW THEATRES

EUROPE became acquainted with the shadow-play through the medium of Italy, while the French brought it into fashion as *ombres chinoises*. Georg Jacob, however, has demonstrated that it is to be met with at a much earlier date in Germany, and England too may make claims to priority. Ben Jonson ends his *Tale of a Tub* with a puppet-play in five scenes which are presented behind a transparent curtain in the manner of a shadow-play. A speaker standing in front with a magician's wand explains the action. In the West the figures are always real pure black shadows, no use being made of the Oriental application of coloured pieces. From the middle of the seventeenth century there is frequent mention of shadow-plays on the German stage—at Danzig in 1683, at Frankfort in 1692—often along with marionettes. The theatre manager Ferdinand Beck, who appeared at Frankfort in 1731, introduced between the acts of his melodramas artistic shadow-plays. In the middle of the eighteenth century a certain Chiarini gave performances of *ombres chinoises* at Hamburg; the figures were attached to strings, at the ends of which rings were tied, the rings going on the fingers of the performer, who manipulated them as if he were playing a piano. The amateur theatres too used to present shadow-plays. In 1781 Goethe got a shadow theatre built in Tiefurt, he himself and

FIG. 353. CHINESE SHADOW-PLAY:
"LE PONT CASSÉ"
French woodcut. About 1830

DOLLS AND PUPPETS

Einsiedel preparing the *libretti* for the performances. The subjects dealt with in these earlier experiments are not now known, for the shadow-play could only get a footing in Germany after it had met with approval in Paris. This type of entertainment seems to have been known in Germany at an early date, but the first record we get of it is in the correspondence of Melchior Grimm on August 15, 1770. In 1775 a certain Ambroise opened

FIG. 354. CHINESE SHADOW-PLAY: PARISIAN TYPES
Beginning of the nineteenth century

a theatre of this kind, which in 1776 gave performances in London. In it was displayed a shipwreck in the midst of thunder and lightning, together with various transformation scenes, including a bridge broken into pieces, a scene which from that time on remained popular in the shadow theatre. From 1784 Dominique Séraphin, with his *ombres chinoises perfectionnées*, was a formidable rival of Ambroise. The former's puppets indicated physical features and dress by thin light strips and were much praised. "The puppets," writes Thiéry, in his *Pariser Führer*,

> represent human deportment very naturally. They dance on a tight rope and execute character dances with the greatest precision. Beasts of all kinds make their appearance here and move in their own special ways, and neither the strings nor the wires which hold and manipulate them can be seen.

FIG. 355. PEEPSHOW AFTER AN ITALIAN ENGRAVING
Beginning of the nineteenth century

FIG. 356. LATERNA MAGICA
French engraving. About 1800

DOLLS AND PUPPETS

Séraphin was much run after, and bore in mind the temper of his period, for from 1789 on he presented only antimonarchical pieces. He died in 1800, but his theatre closed finally only in 1870.

The Romantics loved the shadow theatre as they did the marionettes. Christian Brentano, Achim von Arnim, Justinus Kerner, Tieck, Uhland, and Mörike worked with it, while Count Pocci wrote some pretty pieces for it and designed shadow-figures. Even such an experienced theatre man as Kotzebue

FIG. 357. HOW THE FIGURES OF THE SHADOW THEATRE ARE MOVED BEHIND THE SCENES
French woodcut. About 1840

could not resist its charm. "His large and small shadow-plays," writes Countess Julie Egloffstein in 1817, "are unique in their kind. He has grasped everything that such things possess of the beautiful, and understands the art of producing great things with limited means." In 1827, indeed, there was a regular shadow theatre in Berlin. The great success of the shadow-play between 1760 and 1830 is closely connected with the fashion for silhouettes, which was then at its height. These were worn as pendants, hung on the walls, painted on furniture and crockery; and in the shadow-play they were welcomed in movable form, accompanied even by speech and song. When the new art of lithography pushed the silhouettes aside, and still more when the mechanically produced photograph completely banished for a time all artistic treatment of such things, the shadow theatre also disappeared. In France Eudel, father of the writer Paul

FIG. 358. THE TEA-PARTY
Movable figures from a shadow-play. About 1830
Theater-Museum, Munich

FIG. 359. PICK-A-BACK

FIG. 360. PUNCH WITH A MASK
Movable figure from a shadow-play
About 1830

Theater-Museum, Munich

Eudel, was an artist who still worked for the *ombres chinoises* in a skilful way, but he stood alone. Germany possessed highly gifted designers of silhouettes, such as Konewka, but the shadow-play was forgotten.

Its modern revival is due to French artists. In the Chat Noir, a cabaret started by Rodolphe Salis in 1881, Henri Rivière began to improvise shadow-plays in 1887. Caran d'Ache,

FIG. 361. FROM RIVIÈRE'S SHADOW-PLAY "LA MARCHE À L'ÉTOILE"

Willette, Lucien Métivet, followed him without being able to rival his efforts. Rivière's art provided a fantastic fairy-tale for the eye, deeply poetic in theme, of peculiar beauty in form, the whole a dream which vanished even as one strove to capture it. The artist made use of light and colour to steep his scenes in a mood made arresting through its strange magic. Before him there had been nothing similar to this, and since the Théâtre d'Art vanished, in 1897, nothing to equal it has put in an appearance. Here there were great successions of scenes, such as the *Sphinx*, where the conquerors of all ages passed before the Sphinx, *La Marche à l'Étoile*, where the poor and lonely, beggars, shepherds, and slaves, followed the star of Bethlehem, *Clairs de Lune*, *L'Enfant prodigue*, in which the art of illusion reached its highest and most perfect charm. Rivière added powerfully to the impression created by his work through the utilization of light to emphasize the separate pictures. This was cast through

OCCIDENTAL SHADOW THEATRES

coloured glasses which had to be controlled by ten or twelve men. The Nile landscape floated in a bluish-green twilight, Golgotha flamed forth blood-red, the Sphinx faded into a cold, misty grey, the combination of colour-tones always striking the proper psychological note. Through skilfully handled cutting and diminution Rivière secured astonishing perspective effects by simple means. Nothing is left of all his work now, but even

FIG. 362. FROM L. TIECK'S "ROTKÄPPCHEN"
Schwabing shadow-play, with coloured transparencies by
Dora Brandenburg-Polster

the careful postcard reproductions of his scenes remain yet real things of beauty.

Henri Rivière knew how to present the natural alliance of poetry and painting, to create a fairy-tale theatre which in its possibilities left the regular stage far behind; but his followers did not possess his talents. Hans Schliessmann, who was a native of Mainz, but became an Austrian subject because of his long residence in Vienna, where he had won fame as an illustrator for the comic papers, collaborated with Caran d'Ache in producing shadow-plays at the Vienna Exhibition of Music and the Theatre in 1892, but these had no more than a temporary success. Chronologically the next were the "Elf Scharfrichter" in Munich, who in 1900 introduced shadow-plays in their clever artists' cabaret. In November 1907 Baron Alexander von Bernus sought to revive the shadow-play on a broader basis. This attempt resulted from the æsthetic endeavours of the literary

DOLLS AND PUPPETS

and artistic circle to which Schwabing contributed such a peculiar tone several years before the War. "The shadow theatre," wrote Willy Rath on that occasion, "is intended for those tired of realism; in the shadow is revealed an external simplicity, the truly perfect obstacle to realism." As Bernus himself says: "The shadow theatre reflects in its purest form the intangible world of the waking dream." The stage here was a screen of white linen, 1·15 m. by 90 cm.; the puppets were 35 cm. high,

FIG. 363. FROM L. TIECK'S "ROTKÄPPCHEN"
Schwabing shadow-play, with coloured transparencies by
Dora Brandenburg-Polster

and were brought forward, unseen by the spectators, in strips. They had movable limbs, but the manipulators used restraint in giving them gesture. For illumination the petroleum lamp was preferred to electric light, since the former made the shadow soft and full, and it was possible to graduate the power of the illuminant. The figures were designed by Rolf von Hörschelmann, Dora Polster, Greta von Hörner, Emil Preetorius, and Doris Wimmer. The performances lasted from twenty minutes to an hour and a half, several speakers being engaged in the show. Bernus himself, Karl Wolfskehl, Will Vesper, Paula Rössler, and Adelheid von Sybel wrote the plays, but performances were given also of pieces from older literature, such as Goethe's *Pater Brey*, Mörike's *Letzter König von Orplid*; Justinus Kerner, Tieck, Pocci, and Hans Sach were also represented.

FIG. 364. SCHWABING SHADOW-PLAY
Munich 1907. Prologue to the Turkish shadow-play of
Rolf von Hörschelmann

FIG. 365. FROM WOLFSKEHL'S "WOLF DIETRICH UND DIE RAUHE ELS"
Designed by Rolf von Hörschelmann

FIG. 366. SCENE FROM "DIE SCHILDBÜRGER"
Otto Link. Decoration by C. Tenner

FIG. 367. SCENE FROM "HEILIGE WEIHNACHT"
Otto Link

FIG. 368. OLD GERMANY
Lotte Reininger

FIG. 369. OLD HOLLAND
Lotte Reininger

FIG. 370. OLD FRANCE
Lotte Reininger

FIG. 371. OLD ITALY
Lotte Reininger

FIG. 372. OLD SPAIN
Lotte Reininger

FIG. 373. FROM THE SILHOUETTE FILM "PRINCE ACHMED"
Lotte Reininger

FIG. 374. FROM THE SILHOUETTE FILM "PRINCE ACHMED"
Lotte Reininger

FIG. 375. FROM THE SILHOUETTE FILM "PRINCE ACHMED"
Lotte Reiniger

FIG. 376. FROM THE SILHOUETTE FILM "PRINCE ACHMED"
Lotte Reininger

FIG. 377. FROM THE SILHOUETTE FILM "PRINCE ACHMED"
Lotte Reininger

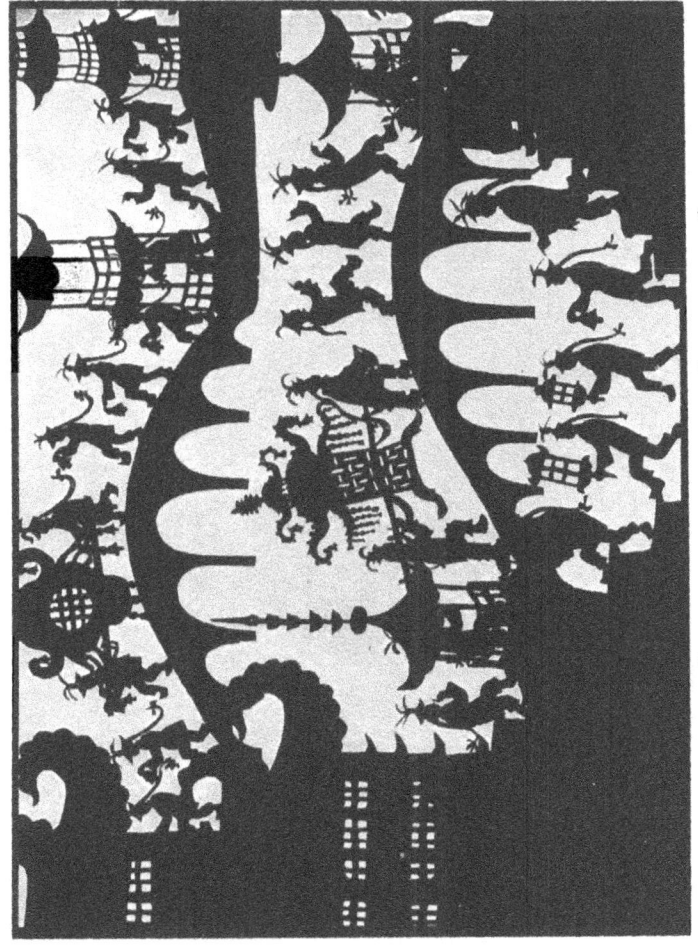

FIG. 378. FROM THE SILHOUETTE FILM "PRINCE ACHMED"
Lotte Reiniger

DOLLS AND PUPPETS

A spinet supplied the music, and both figures and scenery were executed with great refinement; the performances were distinguished and tasteful; the imagination of the audience was aroused to a high degree; but its financial success was not such as to warrant the continuation of this theatre.

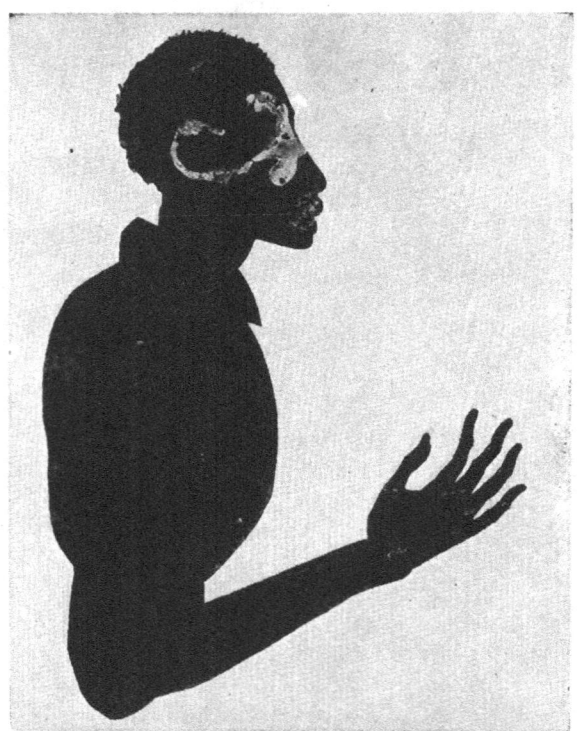

FIG. 379. SHADOW-PLAY FIGURE
Lotte Reiniger

That such novelties should be copied in vulgarized forms in Berlin is comprehensible considering the ceaseless rush for sensations in that great city; such things commonly bear the mark of death on them at the very time of their birth. The Silesian shadow theatre which Friedrich Winckler-Tannenberg and Fritz Ernst opened in the Schiedmeyersaal at Breslau on November 15, 1913, looked as if it were to meet with a friendlier reception. They played *Doctor Faust*, a moral shadow-comedy in three acts adapted from the old *Faust*, Hofmannsthal's *Der Thor und der Tod*, Liliencron's *Die Musik kommt*, and other

FIG. 380. FAUST, SATAN, AND THE FOREST MAIDENS
From the shadow-play *Faust*. Design by Eugen Mirsky, Prague
By permission of the Deutscher Verlag für Jugend und Volk, Vienna

DOLLS AND PUPPETS

pieces, but the War brought this artistic and promising experiment to a premature end. Since then Bruno Zwiener has established a new shadow theatre in Breslau.

The peculiarly imaginative charm of the Javanese *Wajang Purwa* drew German artists too under its spell. Franz Bauer set up a shadow theatre in Bad Lausigk with figures inspired by the Javanese style; Bruno Karberg also gives performances at

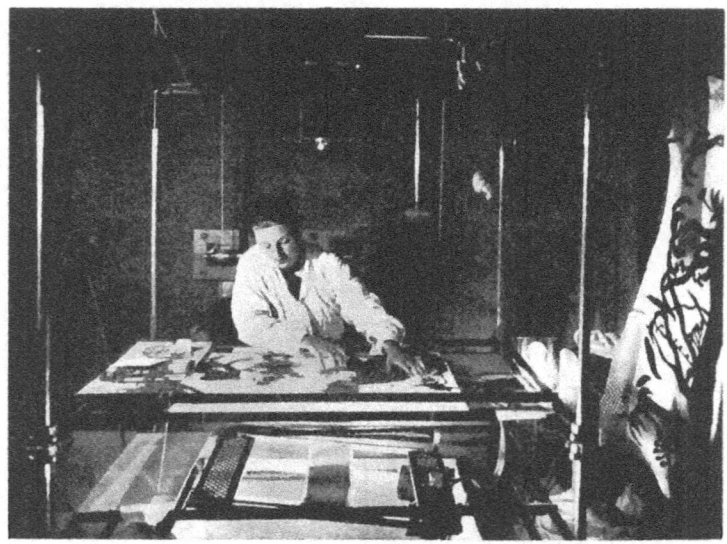

FIG. 381. LOTTE REININGER AT WORK

Hamburg with puppets which are supported, like the Javanese figures, on sticks worked from below. Käthe Baer-Freyer has been influenced by Javanese art in the making of her flat wooden figures, which she paints on one side and manipulates from below. The mystical charm conjured up by the shadow-plays has ever inspired the imaginative artists to further creative activities. Thus, in 1925 Hartlaub got Flaubert's *The Temptation of St Anthony* performed at the Kunsthalle at Mannheim, with shadow-pictures made by Wilfried Otto. Kurt Scheele in Frankfort produced shadow-pictures from the fables of Hans Sachs, songs by Richard Dehmel, and folk-plays; E. H. Bethge designs and writes for the shadow theatre; Eduard Maier goes on tour from Munich with his shadow-plays; Friedrich Winckler-Tannenberg in 1920 sought by means of his *Rakete* to introduce the *Morgenstern* shadow-plays to Berlin.

OCCIDENTAL SHADOW THEATRES

In the winter of 1925 Alfred Hahn at Munich made what seemed to be a most promising start with a shadow-play in colour dealing with the Nativity. Leo Weismantel has established an experimental shadow stage of peculiar interest in that the closely connected arts of the shadow-play and the film are here run together. In Munich Ludwig von Wiech had already put the shadow-play into a film, while Lotte Reiniger with a silhouette-film showed what could be accomplished in this style. *Aladdin's Lamp*, the fairy-tale from *The Arabian Nights*, supplied the theme for *The Story of Prince Achmed* (*Die Geschichte vom Prinzen Achmed*). It was made by the Comenius-Filmgesellschaft, which between 1924 and 1926 must have taken 250,000 separate pictures, of which 100,000 were made use of. By the collaboration of the artist with Karl Koch, Walther Rüttmann, and Berthold Bartosch originated a work of art which on its production at the Volksbühne taught Berlin that this was no mere amusement for æsthetes, but represented new possibilities for the film. A short time ago the Prague silhouette artist Eugen Mirsky also tried this new path which the film has pointed out to the art of the shadow-play. In an exhibition held at Prague in June 1927 he showed silhouette figures which revealed in a peculiar mingling of the arts of the silhouette and the film a new phase, seemingly full of possibilities for the future, of the cinematographic art. His pictures are of no common sort; the step which he has taken from the merely ornamental silhouette to the naturalistic silhouette at all events may open up new prospects to the all too realistic film.

www.ingramcontent.com/pod-product-compliance
Lightning Source LLC
LaVergne TN
LVHW041504070426
835507LV00009B/802